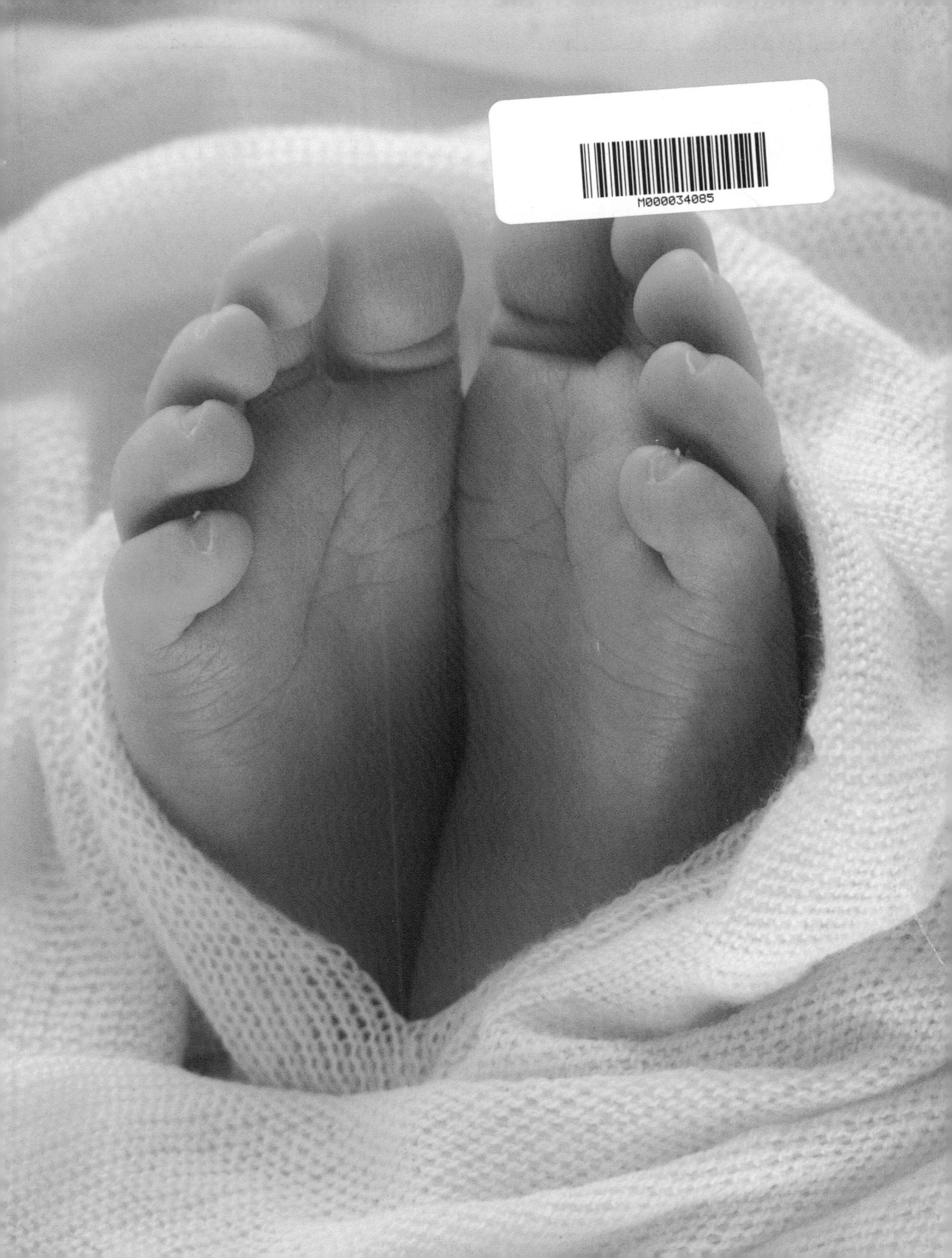

M000034085

Finding out...

My story

My baby's due date

I thought I might be pregnant because

How I felt when the pregnancy was confirmed

Who was with me at the time

Children are love made visible.

American proverb

Who I shared the news with first

Their reaction, thoughts, and feelings

Reaction of family and friends to the news

People who will play an important role throughout my pregnancy

When you were born, you cried and the world rejoiced.

Native American proverb

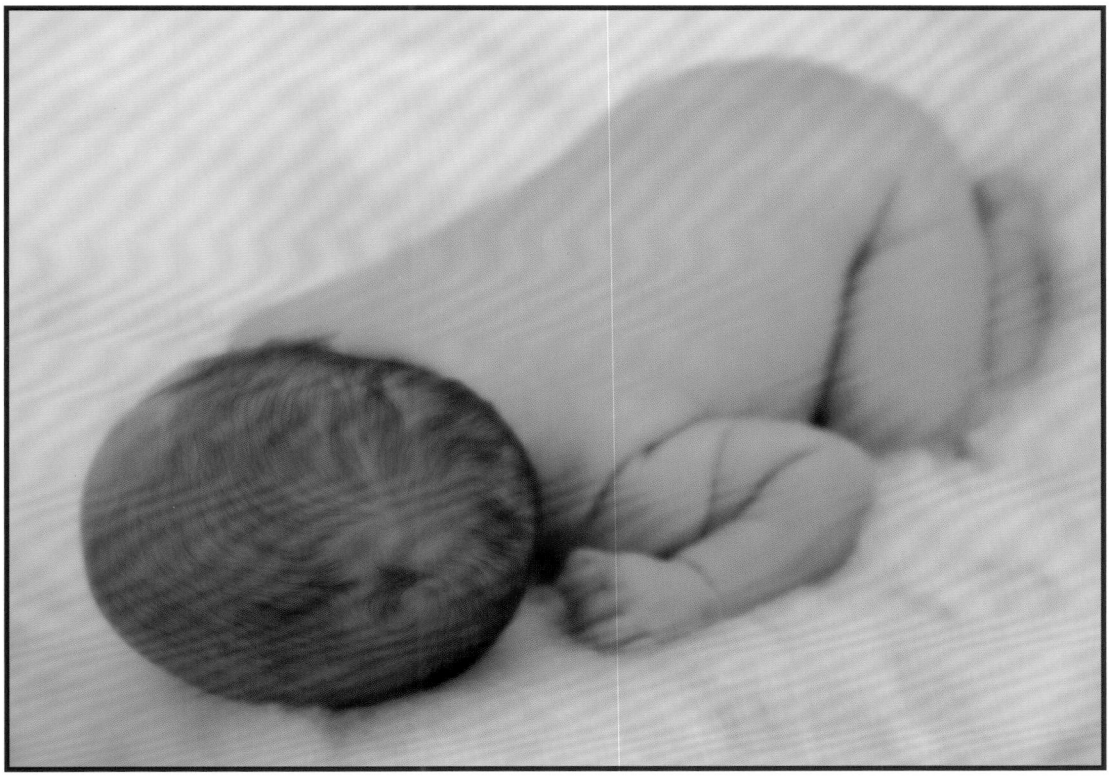

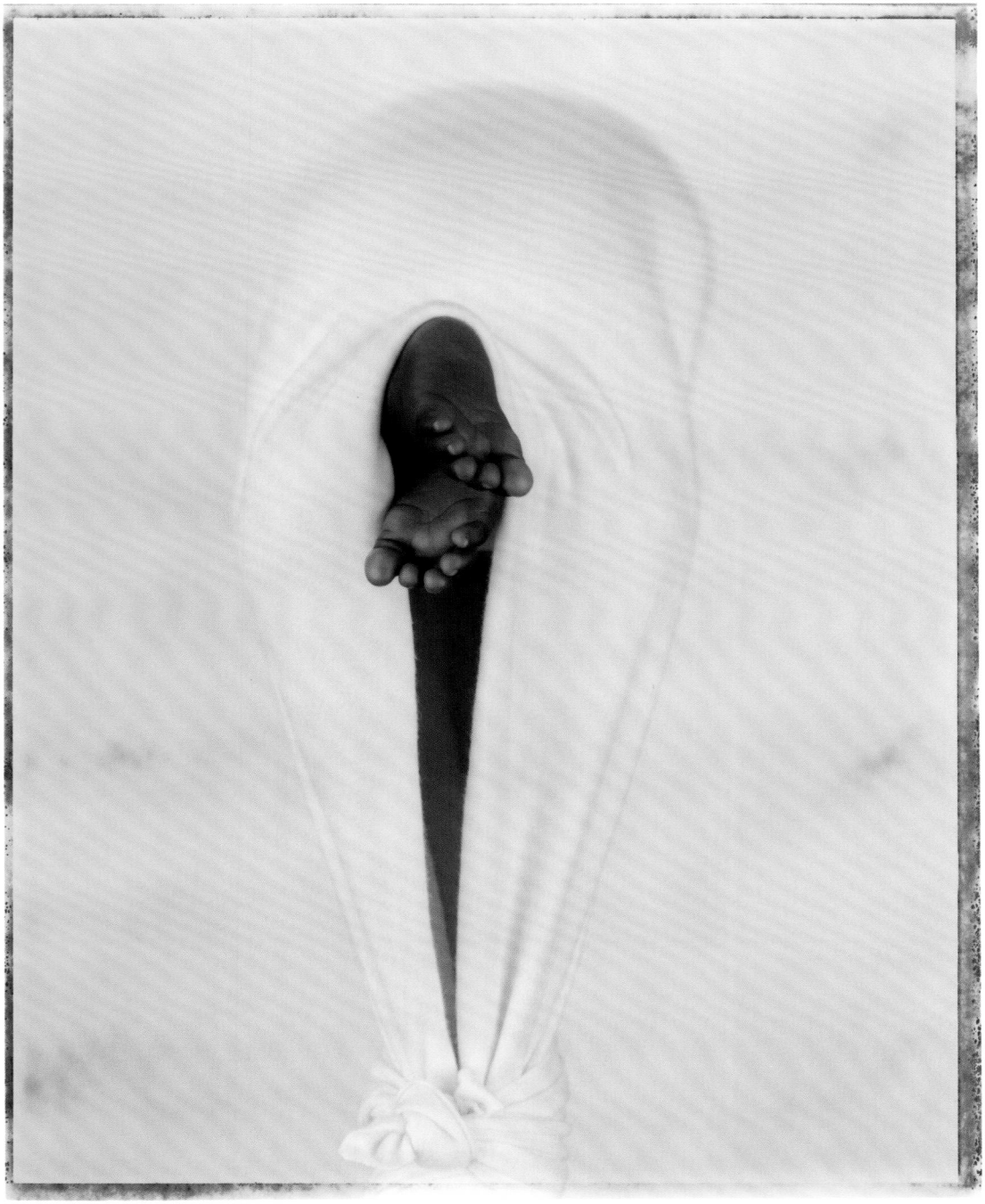

First things first

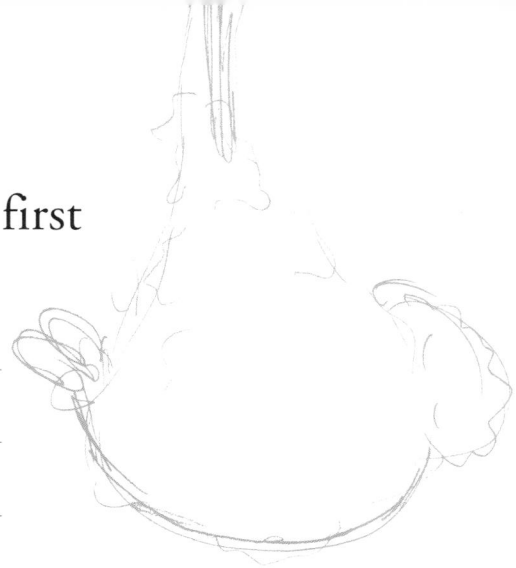

Where I would like to give birth

Who I'd like to be present and why

Mother to be

My thoughts on motherhood

My thoughts on childhood

First doctor or midwife visit

Week

My progress

Baby's progress

Thoughts and feelings about the visit

Mother: the most beautiful word on the lips of mankind.

Kahlil Gibran

Journey through pregnancy

weeks 1 - 12

My body

How I'm feeling about my body

Changes I have noticed

Cravings and aversions

Energy level

A mother's arms are made of tenderness and children sleep soundly in them.

Victor Hugo

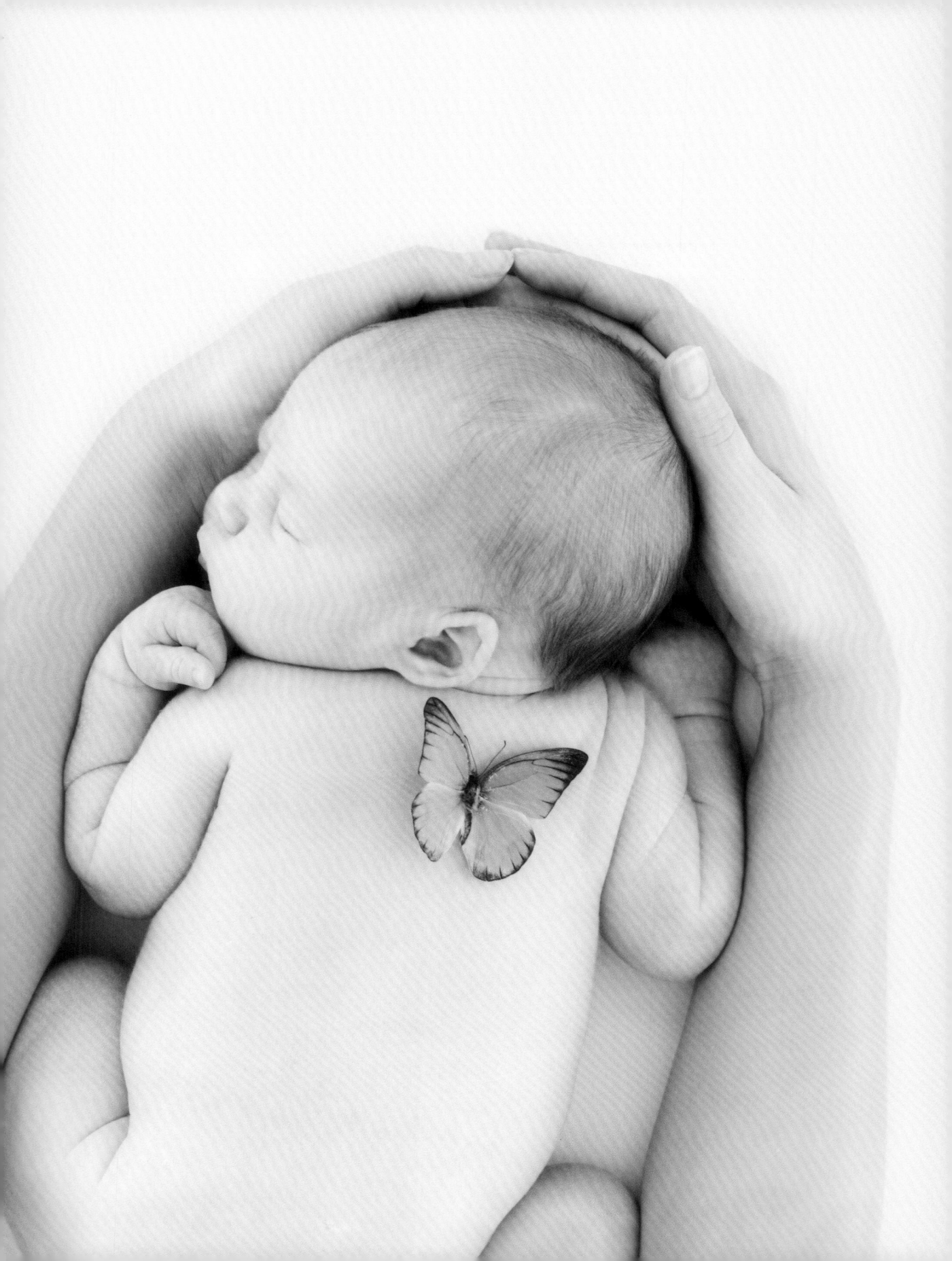

My thoughts

What I'm looking forward to

What I'm hesitant about

What makes me laugh

What makes me cry

A baby is born with a need to be loved – and never outgrows it.

Frank A. Clark

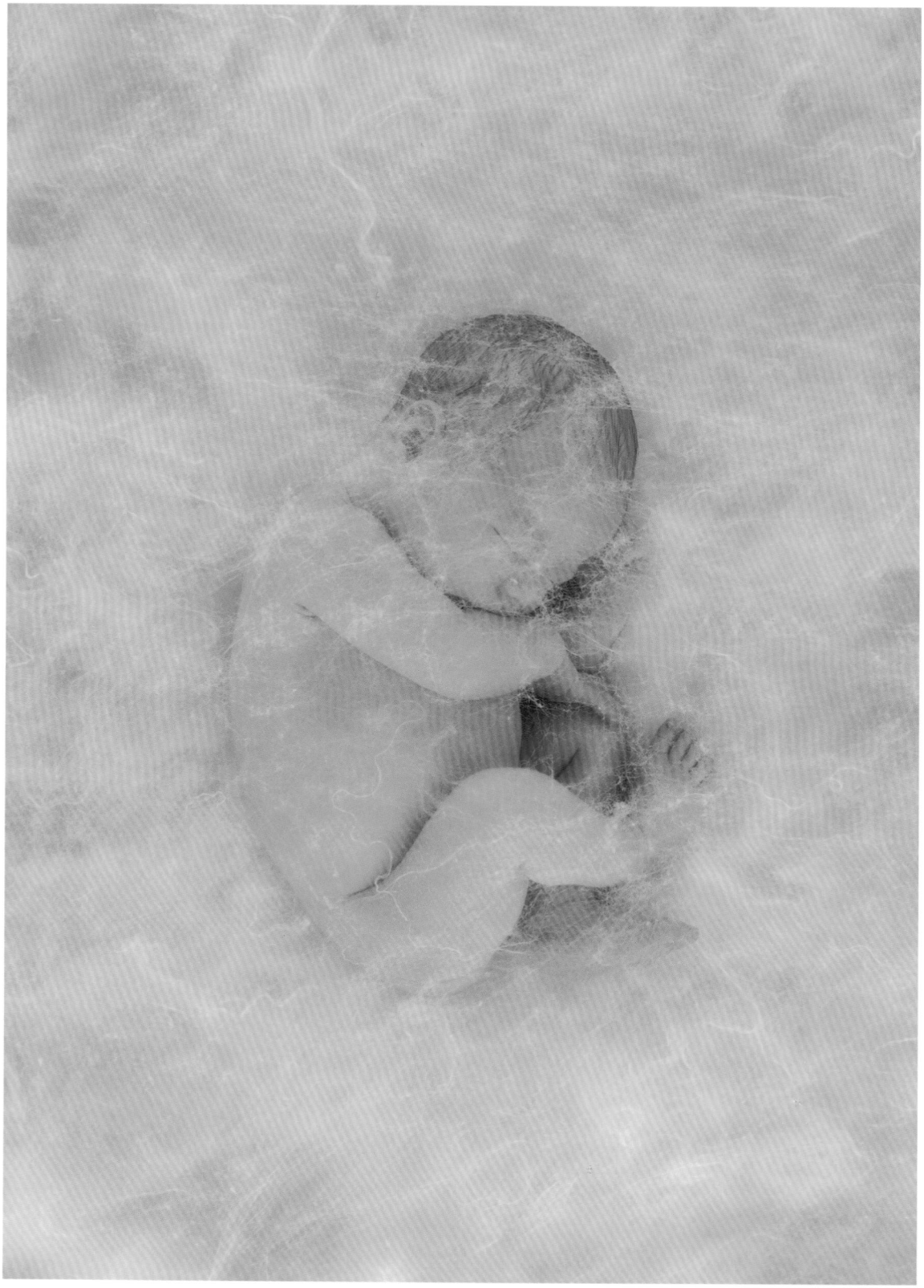

Learning

Interesting things I have learned

Some good advice I received from

Things to remember

My disappearing waistline

weeks 13 - 24

My body

How I'm feeling about my body

Changes I have noticed

Energy level

What I am really enjoying about being pregnant

But this isn't much fun

Date

My weight Tummy width

It was the tiniest thing I ever decided to put my whole life into.

Terri Guillemets

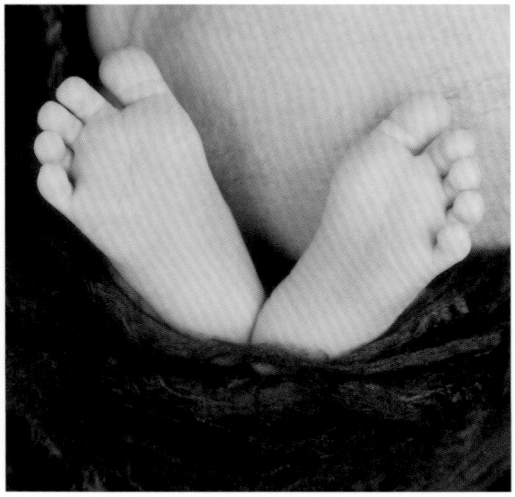

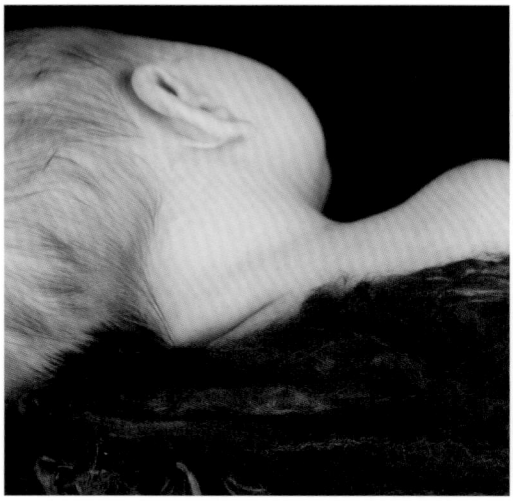

First look

Date/Week _____

Space for ultrasound

What the ultrasound shows _____

_____

_____

_____

My reaction to seeing the baby

Reaction of others who were there

My feelings on finding out the sex of my baby

My feelings on having a girl

My feelings on having a boy

Babies are such a nice way to start people.

Don Herold

Baby's first movements

The physical feeling I had when my baby moved

The emotional feeling I had when my baby moved

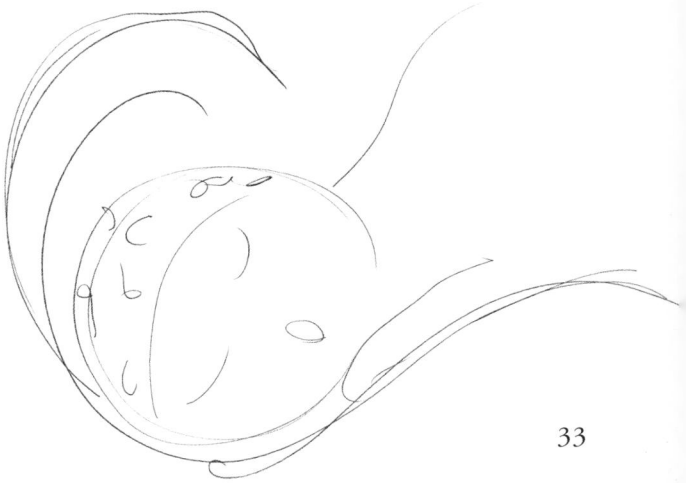

Doctor or Midwife visit

Week

My progress

Baby's progress

Thoughts and feelings about the visit

Keeping up

Information I feel is important to remember

A mother's children are portraits of herself.

Author unknown

All about me

How being pregnant is different from what I expected

How I am feeling about myself and being pregnant

Learning

I am attending childbirth classes at

Thoughts on what I'm learning

Information I feel is important to remember

Friends made and their contact information

The only thing worth stealing is a kiss from a sleeping child.

Joe Houldsworth

Taking care of myself

Things I'm doing now to nurture myself

What I do in my time alone

Things I do to rest

What I'm reading/what I'm learning

Things I'm doing to keep myself strong and healthy

Things I'm doing to prepare my body and mind for labor and delivery

The family is one of nature's masterpieces.

George Santayana

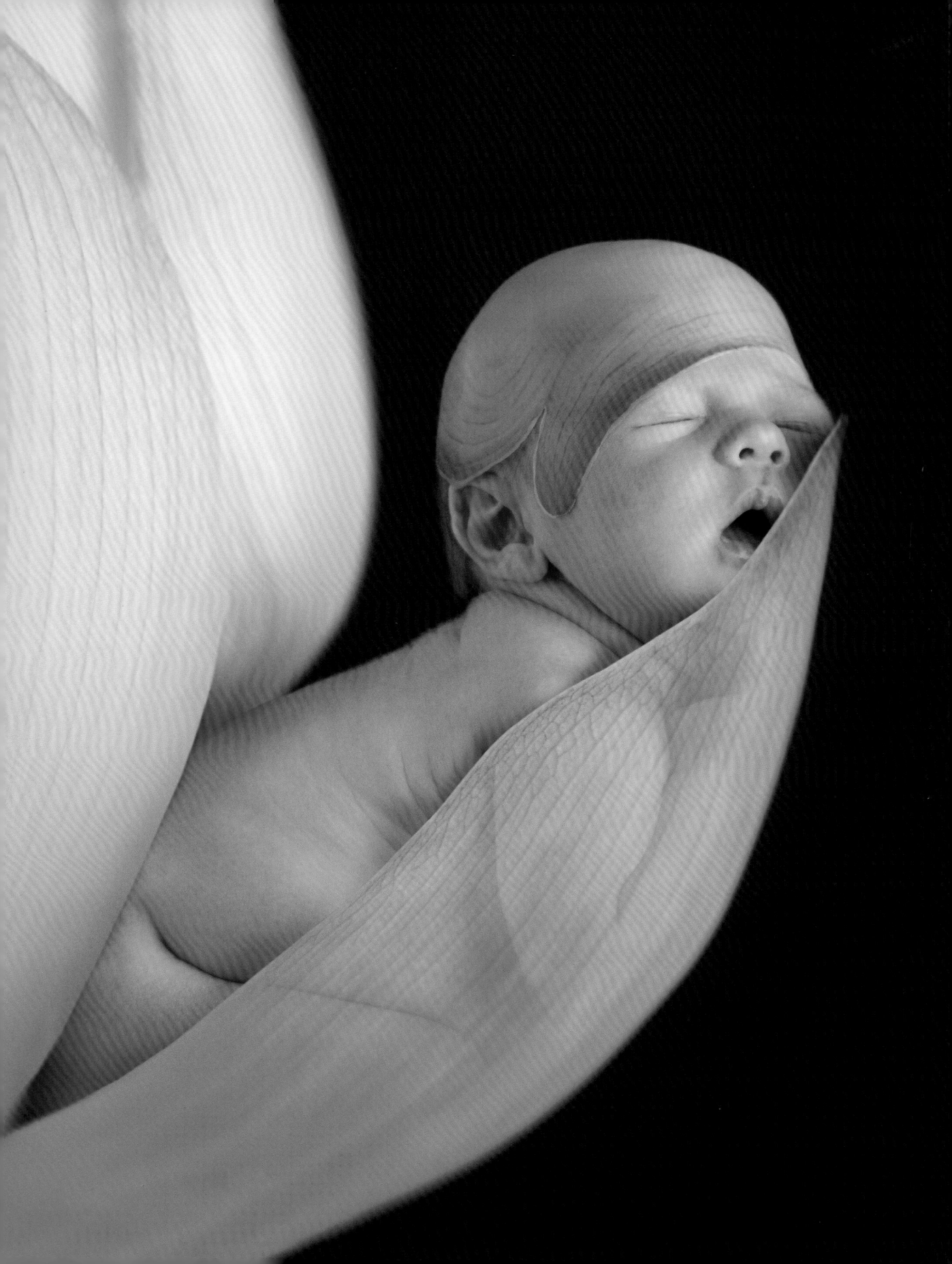

The home stretch

weeks 25 - 40

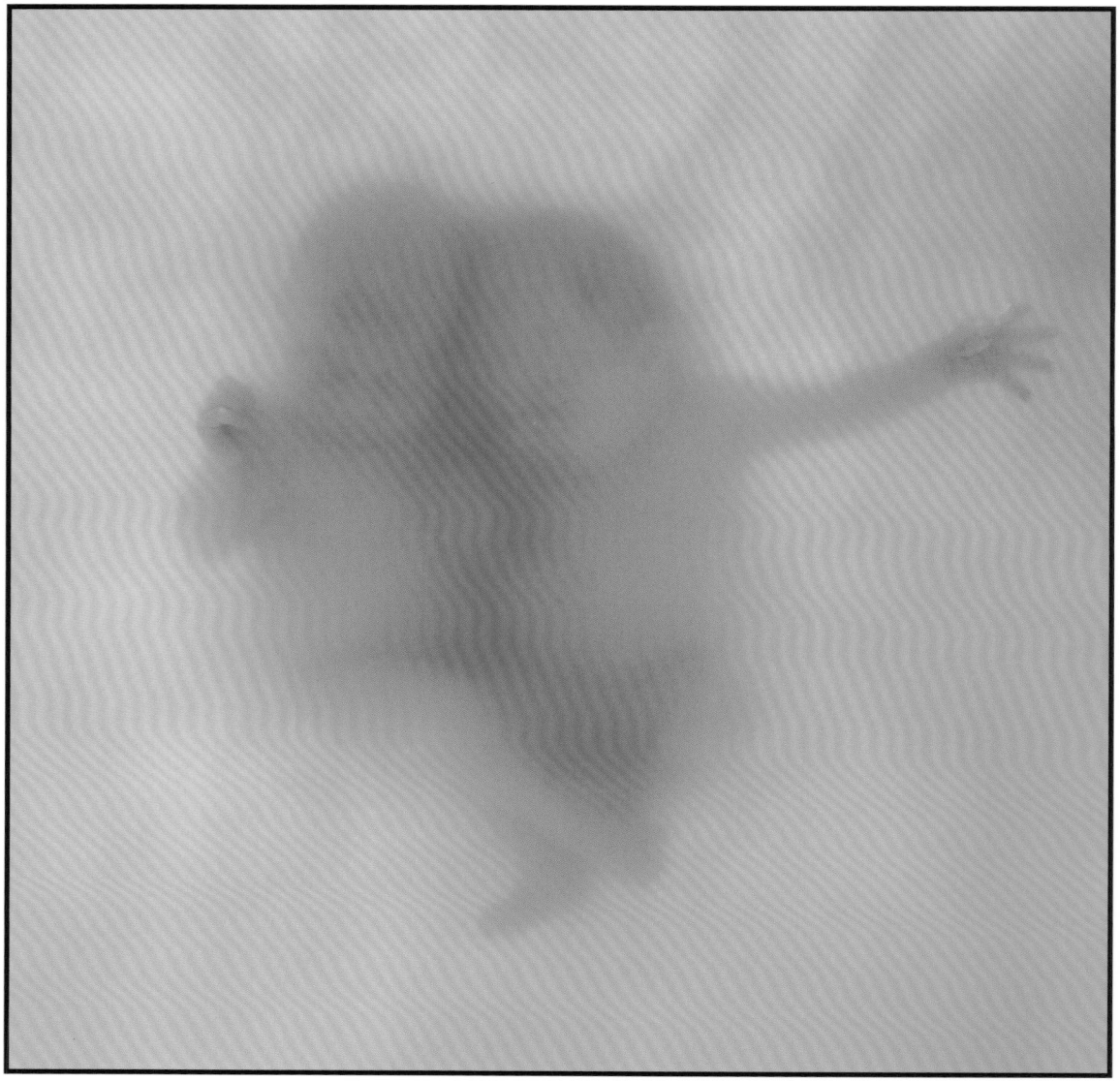

Doctor or Midwife visit

Week

My progress

Baby's progress

Thoughts and feelings about the visit

My body

How I'm feeling about my body

Changes I have noticed

Energy level

What I am really enjoying about being pregnant

But this isn't much fun

Date

My weight Tummy width

Babies are always more trouble than you thought – and more wonderful.

Charles Osgood

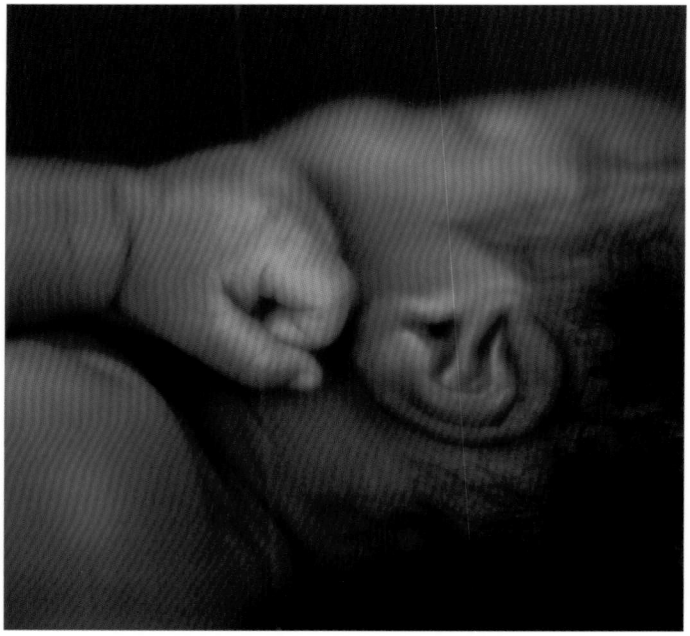

My thoughts

What I'm looking forward to

What I'm hesitant about

What makes me laugh

What makes me cry

Things I'm learning about myself

The soul is healed by being with children.

Fyodor Dostoevsky

Doctor or Midwife visit

Week

My progress

Baby's progress

Thoughts and feelings about the visit

About my baby

My baby is most active

My baby seems to respond to

Special things I enjoy doing for my baby

What I wish most for my baby

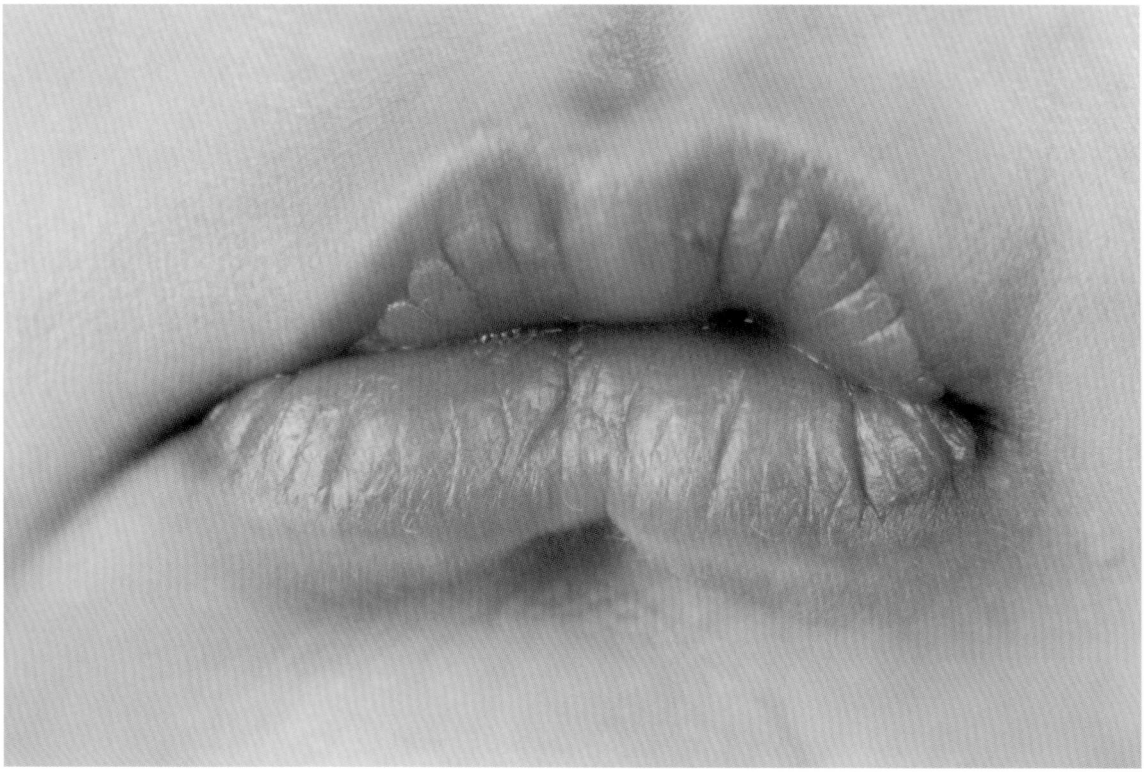

Names

Nicknames for my unborn baby

Boy's names

Girl's names

DRYING
OUT
The Complete Diaper Story

Best guesses

People's comments regarding the sex of my baby

My own feelings about the sex of my baby

For my baby

Special things I have for my baby

Things I still need

Ideas and thoughts on color/theme/feel of nursery

Gifts I have received

Little children are the most lovely flowers this side of Eden.

Rev. Dr Davies

Doctor or Midwife visit

Week

My progress

Baby's progress

Thoughts and feelings about the visit

Looking forward

My thoughts about giving birth

Who I want to support me at the birth

I am excited about

I am anxious about

Special things I would like to have with me at the birth

Every baby needs a lap.

Henry Robin

Dreams

Date

Dream

Thoughts

Date

Dream

Thoughts

Date

Dream

Thoughts

Doctor or Midwife visit

Week

My progress

Baby's progress

Thoughts and feelings about the visit

Special note to my baby

I have been thinking about

I would like you to know

INCHES
CMS

The birth of my baby
congratulations!

My story

I knew I was in labor because

Date and time

Thoughts and feelings

Where I was

Comments about the labor

Who was with me at the birth

Love touched our hearts with tenderness anew, the day
we heard your little voice and cast our eyes on you.

Author unknown

My baby

My baby's name _____

Place of birth _____ Date and time _____

Head circumference _____ Hair color _____

Weight _____ Length _____

My first thoughts and feelings when my baby was born _____

_____

_____

_____

_____

_____

Space for baby's first photo

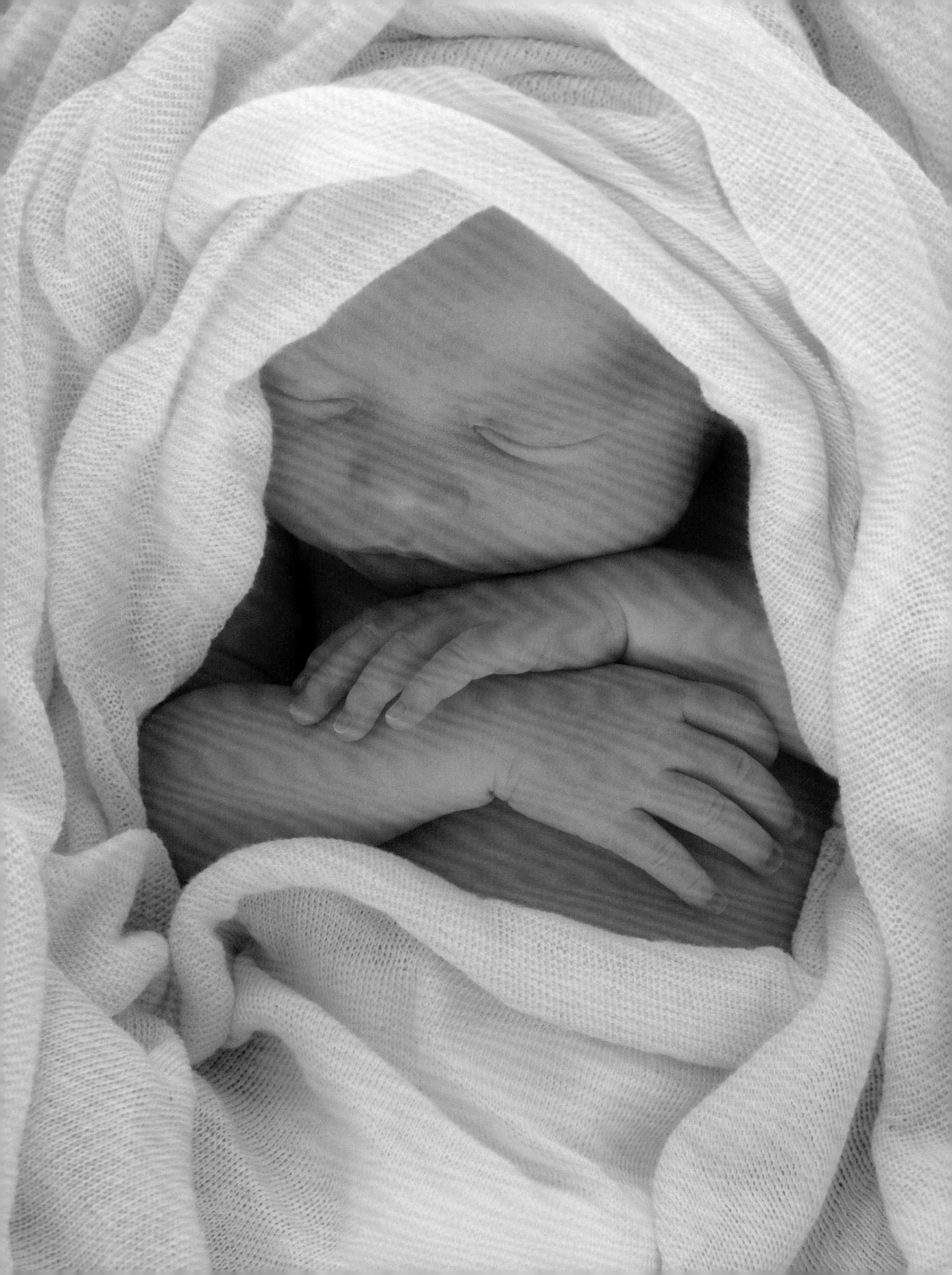

First impressions

Who cried first

My first words to my baby

My biggest surprise about giving birth

Baby's firsts

First feeding

First bath

First diaper change

First calls to share the news

A special note to me

I feel very proud of myself because

Children are likely to live up to what you believe in them.

Lady Bird Johnson

Just me

How my body feels since the delivery

Advice from doctor/midwife

Nursing notes

How it feels not to be pregnant

How it feels to be a mother

My emotions

Going home

Date/time

Baby's outfit

How baby reacted to being home

My thoughts and feelings about bringing baby home

Children are love made visible.

American proverb

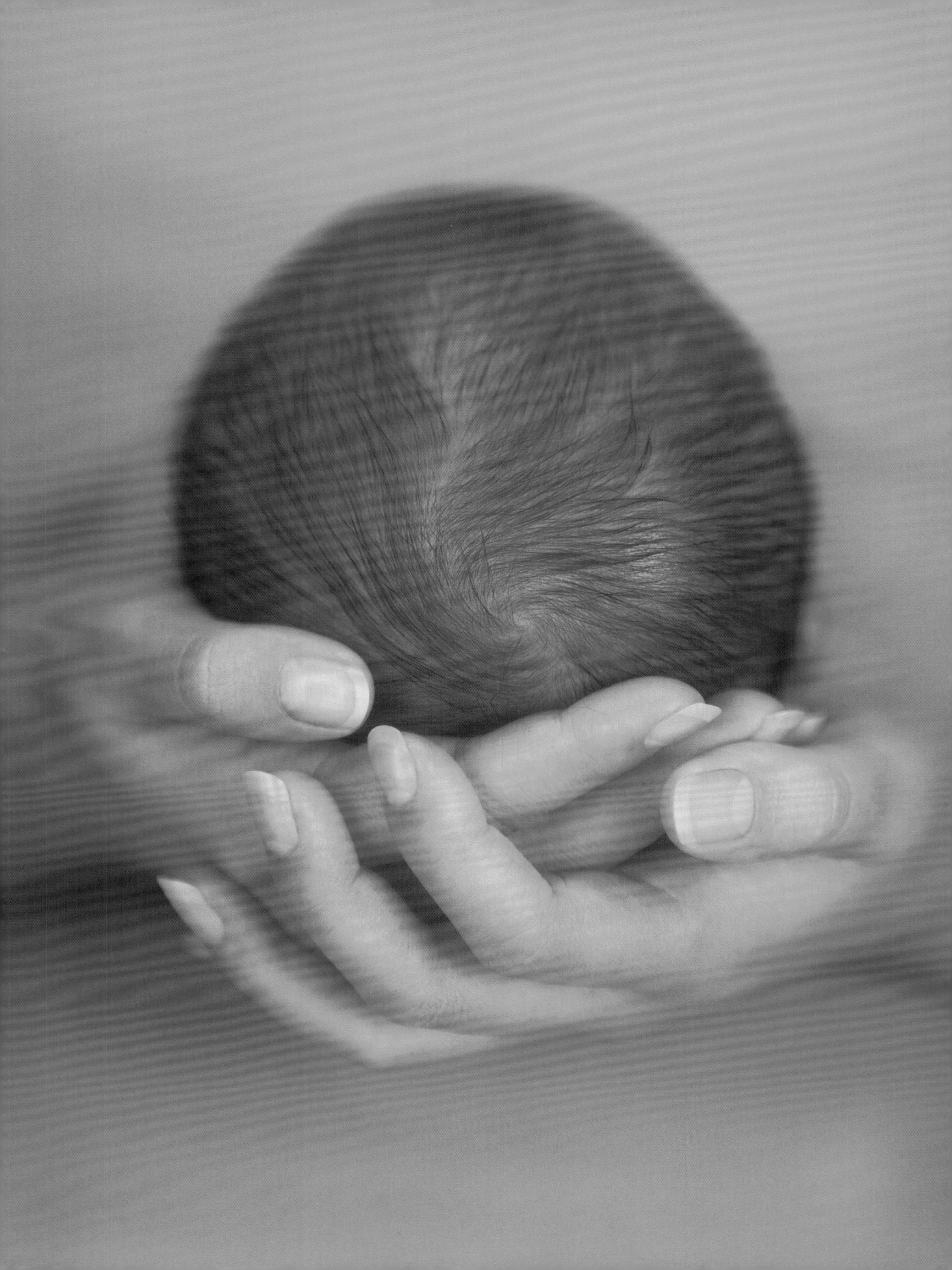

Sleeping arrangements

Adjusting to a new family member

Memorable moments

A new baby is like the beginning of all things –
wonder, hope, a dream of possibilities.

Eda J. Leshan

Settling in

Feeding time

Changing time

Sleepy-time

Baby's disposition

Baby's visitors

Special gifts received

In conclusion

My thoughts and feelings about finishing this book

Last words

Space for family photo

ANNE GEDDES®
www.annegeddes.com

ISBN: 978-1-921652-24-0 - Charlotte Sleeping Cover
ISBN: 978-1-921652-17-2 - Marama & Michael Cover

First published in 2008.
This edition published in 2009 by
Anne Geddes Publishing
Geddes Group Holdings Pty Ltd
Registered Office, Level 9, 225 George Street
Sydney 2000, Australia

© 2008 Anne Geddes

The right of Anne Geddes to be identified as the Author of the Work has been asserted by her in accordance with the Copyright, Designs and Patents Act 1988.

All rights reserved.
No part of this publication may be reproduced, stored in a retrieval system or transmitted in any form or by any means without the prior written permission of the publisher nor be otherwise circulated in any form of binding or cover other than that in which it is published and without a similar condition being imposed on the subsequent purchaser. The author asserts her moral rights in this publication and in all works included in this publication. In particular, the author asserts the right to be identified as the author of the publication and the works herein.

Designed by Kirsten Bryce
Produced by Kel Geddes
Printed in China by 1010 Printing International Limited, China